Waswasah:

The Whispers of Satan

Ibn Qayyim al-Jawziyyah

Waswasah: The Whispers of Satan

Original Arabic Title:

ذم الموسوسين والتحذير من الوسوسة

Author:

Abu Muhammad Abdullah ibn Ahmad ibn Qudamah al-Maqdisi (d. 620 AH)

With commentaries by Ibn Qayyim al-Jawziyyah (d. 751 AH)

English Translation and Edition: Hussein Elasrag

First English Edition: November 2025

Published by Hussein Elasrag

Disclaimer:

This book is for educational and spiritual purposes only. The author, translator, and publisher are not responsible for any misinterpretation or application of the content. Consult qualified scholars for religious rulings. All Quranic verses are translated using the Sahih International edition (quran.com).

Summary

Waswasah: The Whispers of Satan

A Classic Islamic Guide to Combating Obsessive Doubts in Worship.

In the depths of the soul, Satan whispers to divert the believer from the purity of faith. This timeless treatise by Ibn Qudamah al-Maqdisi, completed by Ibn Qayyim al-Jawziyyah, unmasks the devil's traps: excessive scruple in ablutions, doubts in prayer, blameworthy innovations that turn worship into a burden.

Based on the Quran and Sunnah, the book teaches to reject waswasah through certainty and moderation: "Religion is easy, and whoever beautifies it will succeed." Ideal for souls tormented by religious anxiety, it offers spiritual and practical remedy, linking ancestral wisdom to modern challenges.

"A divine antidote to the traps of the shadow."

22 Concise Chapters for Serene Faith.

Revised Edition – Translated and Annotated for the Contemporary Reader.

Keywords :Waswasah, Whispers of Satanm, Ablutions (wudu'), Prayer (salah), Prophetic Sunnah, Religious Scruple, Innovation (bid'ah) Purification (tahara), Doubt (shakk), Serene Faith

Preface

In the name of Allah, the Most Gracious, the Most Merciful.

Praise be to Allah, Who has guided us by His grace and honored us with Muhammad (peace and blessings be upon him) and his message. He encouraged following the Sunnah, emphasizing Allah's love and forgiveness: {Say, "If you should love Allah, then follow me, [so] Allah will love you and forgive you your sins. And Allah is Forgiving and Merciful."} (Al-Imran 3:31). {My mercy encompasses all things. So I will decree it [especially] for those who fear Me and give zakah and those who believe in Our verses— [to] those who follow the Messenger, the unlettered prophet.} (Al-A'raf 7:156-157).

In our time, where the human soul is drowned in a sea of psychological pressures and self-doubts, often called "obsessive-compulsive disorder" or "chronic anxiety" in modern psychology, the book Waswasah: The Whispers of Satan by Imam Abu Muhammad Abdullah ibn Ahmad ibn Qudamah al-Maqdisi (d. 620 AH), enriched by Imam Ibn Qayyim al-Jawziyyah's (d. 751 AH) valuable commentaries, emerges as a gem of Islamic heritage. This short book is not merely a fiqh text addressing satanic whispers in acts of worship such as ablutions, prayer, and purification, but a spiritual guide to liberate the soul from the devil's chains.

Ibn Qudamah wrote this epistle to warn Muslims of Satan's tricks who "will surely sit in wait against them on Your straight path" (Al-A'raf 7:16), enticing them to excess in religion until they despair of Allah's mercy. In our era, where millions suffer from disorders of scrupulosity due to overthinking and perfectionism, this book offers divine therapy, teaching that "certainty is not removed by doubt," and that adherence to the Sunnah is the path to psychological and spiritual peace. It reminds us of the Prophet's saying (peace and blessings be upon him): "If Satan whispers to you in your prayer, say: 'I believe in Allah.'"

In this edited edition, we offer the original text with concise commentaries linking the heritage to contemporary reality, drawing from modern psychological studies such as exposure and response prevention (ERP) theory, which aligns with the Imam's principle of "abandoning the waswasah." I hope this effort is a help for every soul afflicted by whispers, for Allah says: {And whoever fears Allah—He will make for him a way out.} (Al-Talaq 65:2). And Allah is the Best of Planners.

Hussein Elasrag , November 2025

Table of Contents

Chapter 1: The Stratagems of the Devil Employed Against the Children of Adam

Allah has informed us of His enemy Iblis (the Devil) when He questioned him about his refusal to prostrate before Adam. Iblis, in arrogance, claimed superiority over Adam and implored Allah's forgiveness, which He granted. Then Iblis, the sworn enemy of Allah, declared: "[Iblis] said, 'Because You have put me in error, I will surely sit in wait for them on Your straight path. Then I will come to them from before them and from behind them and on their right and on their left, and You will not find most of them grateful [to You].'" (Al-A'raf 7:16-17).

Most Quranic exegetes explain that Satan's response was deliberately phrased to emphasize his determination to plot against the believers. Ibn 'Abbas said: "The straight path refers to the manifest religion of Allah, Islam." Ibn Mas'ud declared: "It is the Book of Allah, the Quran." Jabir ibn 'Abdullah affirmed: "It is Islam." Mujahid specified: "It is the truth." These are synonymous expressions denoting one reality: the path to Allah.

Sabrah ibn Abi Fakih reported that the Prophet (peace and blessings be upon him) said: "Satan lies in wait for the children of Adam with all his tricks."

Ibn 'Atiyah reports from Ibn 'Abbas that "before them" means Satan intervenes in their worldly affairs. 'Ali ibn Abi Talhah reported that the verse means: "I will sow doubt in them about the Hereafter." This concurs with al-Hasan's narration, where Satan seeks to make believers deny the Resurrection, Paradise, and Hell. Mujahid interpreted "before them" as "from the direction they face, presenting his temptations visibly."

As for what happens behind them, Ibn 'Abbas explained: "I will incite them to covet the fleeting pleasures of this illusory world." Al-Hasan added: "I will adorn the things of this world for them." Abu Salih said: "I will make them deny the Hereafter and turn away from it." Ibn 'Abbas specified: "I will sow doubt about the value of their faith and good deeds." Al-Hasan noted: "I will divert them from pious acts."

Regarding "on their right and left," al-Hasan said: "I will command them to commit evil and make it appealing to their eyes." Ibn 'Abbas authentically reported: "Satan omitted 'from above' because he knows that Allah is above them." Ash-Sha'bi remarked: "Allah grants them His mercy from above." Qatadah declared: "O children of Adam, Satan approaches you from all sides except from above, so he cannot prevent Allah's mercy from reaching you."

Al-Wahidi noted: "Some say the right represents good deeds and the left bad ones, as the Arabs say: 'Place me on your right but not on your left,' meaning 'Make me one of your closest allies, not the farthest.'"

Al-Azhari, citing scholars, reports that Iblis swore by Allah's power: "[Iblis] said, 'By Your might, I will surely mislead them all.'" (Sad 38:82), leading them to deny the stories of past nations, their resurrection, and sowing confusion in daily affairs. Abu Ishaq and al-Zamakhshari (according to Abu Ishaq) emphasized: "These instructions accentuate the threat: 'I will assault them from all sides.' Allah knows best—this guarantees their misguidance from all directions." Al-Zamakhshari interpreted: "Enemies usually attack from four sides." This illustrates Satan's pervasive whispers and influence. Allah said to him: "And incite [to senselessness] whoever you can among them with your voice and assault them with your horses and foot soldiers and become a partner in their wealth and children and promise them." (Al-Isra' 17:64).

Shaqiq ibn Ibrahim said: "Every morning, Satan ambushes me from four different observation points—front, back, right, left—whispering: 'Don't fear, Allah is Forgiving and Merciful.' I recite: {Indeed, I am the Perpetual Forgiver of whoever repents and believes and does righteousness and then continues in guidance.} (Ta-Ha 20:82). If he approaches from behind to sadden me about what I leave behind at death, I recite: {And there is no creature on [or within] the earth or bird that flies with its wings except [that they are] communities like you. We have not neglected in the Register a thing.} (Al-An'am 6:38). From the right, to incite desire for women, I recite: {Blessed is the destiny of the virtuous.} (Al-A'raf 7:128). From the left, to kindle all desires, I recite: {And there will be a partition between them and what they desire.} (Saba' 34:54)."

In summary, humanity follows one of four directions: right, left, front, back, and Satan lurks in each. If one follows Allah's commands,

Satan erects obstacles to obedience; if one turns to sin, he aids and encourages.

This is corroborated by Allah's words: "And We have assigned to them companions who made attractive to them what was before them and what was behind them [i.e., the worst of them]." (Fussilat 41:25). Al-Kalbi explained: "We assigned them devilish companions." Muqatil said: "We prepared devilish allies for them." Ibn 'Abbas specified: "Before them: preoccupations of this world; behind: matters of the Hereafter."

They embellished this world to their eyes until they preferred it over the Hereafter, even denying it. Al-Kalbi added: "They idealized denying the Hereafter—no Paradise, no Hell, no Resurrection—and the misguidance of the world." Ibn Zayd said: "They normalized past and future sins, preventing repentance."

Satan acts from all sides, targeting this world and the Hereafter; he uses the angel inciting to good (on the right) to hinder virtue, and the one forbidding evil (on the left) to encourage vice. This culminates in these words: "[Iblis] said, 'By Your might, I will surely mislead them all.'" (Sad 38:82) and "They invoke not besides Him other than female [deities], and they [in fact] invoke not except Satan, a rebel. Allah has cursed him; and he said, 'I will surely take from among Your servants a specific portion. And I will mislead them and I will arouse in them [sinful] desires, and I will command them so they will slit the ears of cattle, and I will command them so they will change the creation of Allah.' And whoever takes Satan as an ally instead of Allah has certainly sustained a clear loss. He promises them and tempts them with hope, but Satan does not promise them except delusion." (An-Nisa' 4:117-120).

Ad-Dahhak: "A specific portion is a fixed share of Allah's servants." Al-Zajjaj: "A portion I claim for myself." Al-Farra': "Those over whom he exercises authority."

In truth, it is an estimation: obeying Satan costs one his portion; humanity divides between Satan's followers and those guided by Allah. {I will mislead them} away from the truth; {I will arouse in them [sinful] desires}: Ibn 'Abbas: "By preventing repentance." Al-Kalbi: "By denying Paradise, Hell, and the Resurrection." Al-Zajjaj: "By misleading while denying the Hereafter's fortune."

Another possibility: inciting sinful impulses and religious innovations, or excessive attachment to the world at the expense of the Hereafter.

{Command them to slit the ears of cattle}—the ear-marking of the Bahirah (dedicated animal), according to most exegetes. Scholars extend this to ear-piercing for ornament only for girls, citing Aisha's hadith about Umm Zar': "He gave me many ornaments; my ears are heavy from them." The Prophet replied: "I am to you what Abu Zar' was to Umm Zar'." Imam Ahmad permitted it for girls, but not boys.

{And I will command them to change the creation of Allah}: Ibn 'Abbas: "Satan meant Allah's religion." Consensus of Ibrahim, Mujahid, al-Hasan, etc. Allah created His servants according to their fitrah (innate Islam): {So direct your face toward the religion, inclining to truth. [Adhere to] the fitrah of Allah upon which He has created [all] people. No change should there be in the creation of Allah. That is the correct religion, but most of the people do not know. [Adhere to it], turning in repentance to Him, and fear Him and establish prayer and do not be of those who associate others with Allah.} (Ar-Rum 30:30-31).

The Prophet said: "Every child is born upon the fitrah, then his parents make him a Jew, Christian, or Magian. If a beast gives birth to a young one intact, do you see any mutilation?" Then he recited: "The fitrah of Allah upon which He has created [all] people."

The Prophet linked altering the fitrah (by parental influence) to modifying creation (mutilation)—the acts Satan promises: polytheism corrupts the fitrah; mutilation alters the form.

He promises them and tempts them with hopes; these promises penetrate hearts: "Your life will extend to satisfy your desires; attain a rank superior to your kin and enemies." Satan inflates hope with lies, arousing unattainable desires. Difference: promises are pure lies; hopes are illusory pursuits. The corrupted soul feeds on satanic illusions, thriving on false optimism.

Allah says: "Satan promises them and tempts them with hope, but Satan does not promise them except delusion." (An-Nisa' 4:120). "Satan threatens you with poverty and orders you to immorality, but Allah promises you forgiveness from Him and bounty." (Al-Baqarah 2:268). "Immortality" here means stinginess (per context). Muqatil and al-Kalbi: The Quranic term "fahsha" usually denotes adultery, but here stinginess. Correct interpretation: It refers to evil deeds in general, encompassing all vices. Satan commands sins (including stinginess) and threatens ruin for good.

Thus, Satan demands: divert virtue from its purpose; command vice, adorned for ease. Allah responds with forgiveness (shield against evil) and bounty (reward for good).

From 'Abdullah ibn Mas'ud, the Prophet (peace and blessings be upon him) said: "Satan flows through the son of Adam like blood, just as the angel does. Satan's blood flows with bad promises and lies. The angel's blood flows with good promises and affirms truth. He who hears good promises praises Allah; he who hears the opposite seeks refuge from the accursed Satan." He recited: "Satan threatens you with poverty and orders you to immorality" (Al-Baqarah 2:268).

Angels and devils contend for the heart like night and day.

Chapter 2: The Diabolical Insinuations of Satan

One of Satan's main tricks is to instill doubt in the hearts of Muslims regarding acts of ritual purification—such as ablutions—and prayer, precisely when they are about to perform them. Through these whispers, he diverts them from the Prophet's Sunnah, convincing them that the established teachings are insufficient for worshiping Allah properly. In their misguided zeal, they invent new methods, believing they will increase their divine reward; in reality, such innovations diminish it, or nullify it entirely.

It is beyond doubt that Satan incites people to embrace perverse ideas and succumb to temptations. It is the heedless who respond to his call, submit to his influence, and execute his designs. They reject the Prophet's Sunnah to such an extent that an afflicted person might claim that even ablutions performed exactly as the Prophet did—with the same washing—do not achieve true purity.

The Prophet (peace and blessings be upon him) performed his ablutions (wudu') with only a quarter of a ratl of Syrian water (about half a liter), and for the ghusl (full ritual bath), he used one and a quarter ratls (about one and a half liters). Yet, one seduced by evil temptations considers this insufficient, even for rinsing the hands. It is authentically reported that the Prophet performed each step of the ablutions successively, limiting himself to three washings at most for each, and he said: "Whoever overdoes it harms himself and transgresses."

Thus, the one targeted by insinuations is himself a transgressor, as the Prophet attested. How, then, can such excesses draw one closer to God when they transgress the limits He has set?

It is also reported that the Prophet performed ghusl with Aisha (may Allah be pleased with her) in a single large vessel, its walls still coated with dough residue. If Satan, possessed by evil, heard of such a practice, he would protest: "This barely suffices for two people to purify properly!"

The Prophet shared this vessel not only with Aisha, but also with wives like Maymunah and Umm Salama. Ibn Umar reported: "In the time of the Prophet, spouses performed ablutions from a single vessel."

The Prophet's teachings confirm that it is permissible to wash in any vessel, even if not full. Whoever waits for the basin to overflow for ablutions or refuses to share it transgresses the Sunnah.

Shaykh al-Islam Ibn Taymiyyah (may Allah have mercy on him) observed: "Reprimanding those who legislate outside Allah's divine Law requires greater firmness, for they worship Him with their inventions, abandoning the Sunnah of His Messenger." This authentic Sunnah attests that the Prophet and his Companions avoided wasting water, as did their successors.

Sa'id ibn al-Musayyib (may Allah have mercy on him) said: "I performed my ablutions with a single vessel, leaving a little water for my wife." Imam Ahmad (may Allah have mercy on him) advised: "The scholar uses little water."

During his ghusl, the Prophet dipped his hand into the vessel to rinse his mouth and nostrils. Those suffering from mental disturbances reject this gesture, deeming the water impure and refusing to share it with their wife, showing repulsion like that of a disbeliever toward Allah's Name.

The afflicted may retort: "These are precautions taken in the name of religion, following the Prophet's words: 'Leave what makes you doubt for what does not make you doubt,' 'Avoid suspicions to preserve faith and honor,' and 'Sin is what troubles the soul.'"

The early scholars noted: "Sin engenders anxiety in the heart." The Prophet, passing by a date on the road, said: "If I did not fear it was charity, I would have eaten it." Did he not abstain out of precaution?

Fatwa of Imam Malik: In case of doubt regarding the first or third pronouncement of divorce, consider the third as valid to avoid illicit relations. If you forget which wife you divorced, the divorce applies to all your wives, as a precaution. If you say: "The divorce is final at the end of the year," it takes effect immediately, preventively.

Scholars' advice: A stain of impurity not found on a garment? Wash it entirely. Clean clothes, unidentified impure garment? Pray in it and add an extra prayer for certainty. Clean vessels mixed with impurities? Avoid all and perform tayammum. Doubt about the Qibla direction? Some advise praying four times for certainty. Forgot a daytime prayer? Repeat all five.

The Prophet ruled: In case of doubt during prayer, act according to your certainty (e.g., referring to the Qibla). Prohibit hunting if uncertain of the hunter or risk of drowning.

These examples illustrate caution in the face of doubt. Islam advocates a precaution based on certainty, even if labeled "insinuation"!

Precaution—which consists of preferring certainty over doubt and guarding against suspicion—is in accordance with the Sharia, not the blameworthy innovation. It is preferable to heedless laxity that neglects the amount of water, place of prayer, or purity of clothes, and considers everything pure despite doubt.

They retort: "The objections target our safeguards in obligations and prohibitions—preferable to laxity breeding neglect of duties and encroachment on prohibitions."

Allah says: {There has certainly been for you in the Messenger of Allah an excellent pattern for anyone whose hope is in Allah and the Last Day and [who] remembers Allah often.} (Al-Ahzab 33:21). {Say, "If you love Allah, then follow me,

[so] Allah will love you and forgive you your sins. And Allah is Forgiving and Merciful."} (Al-Imran 3:31). {Follow him that you may be guided.} (Al-A'raf 7:158). {This is My way, which is straight, so follow it; and do not follow [other] ways.} (Al-An'am 6:153).

Allah's straight path is that of the Prophet, followed by the Companions. Deviation is transgression, major or minor, whose gravity Allah alone judges.

The Prophet's Sunnah and that of his Companions discern good from evil. Transgressors—oppressors, mujtahids, or muqallids—are sometimes punished, forgiven, or rewarded according to their intentions and efforts.

The prophetic guidance, transmitted by the Companions, indicates the path to follow. Recall Islam's prohibition of superfluity and extravagance; moderation and adherence to the Sunnah are essential.

Allah commands: {O People of the Scripture, do not commit excess in your religion or say about Allah except the truth.} (An-Nisa' 4:171). {And do not throw [yourselves] with your [own] hands into destruction [by disobedience].} (Al-Baqarah 2:195). {And do not tie your hand [to your neck] and do not extend it completely.} {These are the limits of Allah, so do not approach them.} (Al-Baqarah 2:187). {And do not transgress. Indeed, Allah does not like transgressors.} (Al-Baqarah 2:190). {Invoke your Lord in humble submission and in private. Indeed, He does not like transgressors.} (Al-A'raf 7:55).

Ibn 'Abbas: On the morning of Al-Aqabah, the Prophet, mounted on a camel, said to me: "Pick up pebbles." I took seven; he shook them: "Wash these intruders." Then: "Beware of excess in religion; previous nations perished by excess."

Anas: The Prophet warned: "Do not harden yourselves, lest difficulty harden against you.

Austere nations suffered divine austerity; some remained in monasteries." Citation: {Then We sent following their footsteps Our messengers and followed [them] with Jesus, the son of Mary, and gave him the Gospel. And We placed in the hearts of those who followed him compassion and mercy and monasticism, which they innovated; We did not prescribe it for them except [that they did so] seeking the approval of Allah. But they did not observe it with due observance. So We gave the ones who believed among them their reward, but many of them are defiantly disobedient.} (Al-Hadid 57:27).

The Prophet forbade all excessive religious rigor, noting that voluntary austerity attracts divine trials or decreed ones. Austerity according to Sharia: binding vows. Decreed: satanic whispers.

Al-Bukhari: "Scholars abhorred ablutions excessive beyond the prophetic norm." Ibn 'Umar: "Correct ablutions are synonymous with purity."

Fiqh embodies religious sobriety and fidelity to the Sunnah. 'Ubayy ibn Ka'b: "Follow the Prophet's path and Sunnah; the disciple remembers Allah, his body trembles in fear, sins fall like autumn leaves. The sobriety of the Sunnah prevails over excessive interpretation. Align sobriety with prophetic practice."

Shaykh Abu Muhammad al-Maqdisi, in Dham al-Muwaswisin: "Praise Allah for guiding us by His grace, honoring Muhammad's message. He encouraged following the Sunnah, emphasizing Allah's love and forgiveness: {Say, 'If you love Allah, follow me. Allah will love you and forgive your sins. Allah is Forgiving and Merciful.'} (Al-Imran 3:31). {My mercy encompasses all things. I decree it for those who fear Me, give zakah, believe in Our verses—those who follow the Messenger, the unlettered prophet} (Al-A'raf 7:156-157). Believe in Allah and His Messenger, the unlettered prophet who believes in Allah and His words; follow him to be guided."

Allah made Satan the enemy of man, assailing the Straight Path from all sides: {My Lord, because You have made me err, I will surely make [disobedience] attractive to them on Your path...} (Al-A'raf 7:16-17).

Allah warns against Satan's path and commands enmity: {Indeed, Satan is an enemy to you; so take him as an enemy.} (Fatir 35:6). {O children of Adam, let not Satan tempt you as he removed your parents from Paradise.} (Al-A'raf 7:27).

Allah related Satan's act against Adam and Eve to incite obedience, leaving no excuse for their followers. He commands following the Straight Path, forbidding deviation: {This is My way, which is straight, so follow it; and do not follow [other] ways.} (Al-An'am 6:153).

Allah's straight path: that of the Prophet and his Companions. {Ya Seen. By the wise Quran. Indeed you, [O Muhammad], are from among the messengers, [Who is] on a straight path.}

(Ya Sin 36:1-4). {You are certainly, by the favor of your Lord, on a straight path.} (Al-Hajj 22:54). {And you, [O Muhammad], are only a guide.} (Ash-Shura 42:52).

The Prophet's followers follow the Straight Path, deserving love and forgiveness of their sins. Deviants: innovators, following Satan's path, deprived of the promised mercy.

Those influenced by whispers obey Satan, rejecting the prophetic Sunnah and the community's Sunnah. This blind obedience leads them to believe prophetic ablutions and prayer are invalid. Sharing children's meals or common dishes (Muslim norm) is deemed impure. Satan's influence blinds, for sophists deny creation, senses, and self-knowledge. They wash, recite, listen, yet doubt reality! Satan sows doubt on intentions despite heart certainty, contesting this certainty with whispers—an excessive obedience leading to total submission.

Whispered: Accepting perversion, self-destruction: plunging into cold, eye-irritating baths.

From Abu al-Faraj ibn al-Jawzi, reported by Abu al-Wafa' ibn 'Uqayl: A man asked: "I dip my finger multiple times in the sack, doubting its wetness; what say you?" Shaykh: "Prayer ascends from you." "Why?" "The Prophet: Three states not reported: the mad until reason, the sleeper until waking, the child until puberty." Repeated dipping with doubt is a sign of madness.

Ibn Qudamah: "Satan preoccupies until the congregation is missed or the intention loop delays the takbir, losing a rak'ah."

Reported: Severely afflicted person, obsessed with incessant verbalization of niyyah: "I pray... such and such prayer."

Satan torments earthly souls before the Hereafter, pushing extremes taken for piety by straying from the Sunnah.

To escape perdition, find truth in the Prophet's words and deeds. Affirm the straight path; beware others, satanic traps. Satan: declared enemy, attracts evil: {He only invites his adherents to be among the companions of the Blaze.} (Fatir 35:6).

Abandon opposites to the Sunnah; doubting the Prophet's path risks unbelief. Imitate the Companions/Tabi'in: Ibrahim an-Nakha'i: "My predecessors, if I had not washed my nails, I would not do so either."

Zayn al-'Abidin to his son: "Go fetch a garment for your needs; flies soil clothes." Remembering the limit of two garments imposed on the Prophet and Companions, he withdrew.

'Umar ibn al-Khattab, determined to act, renounced: "The Prophet did not do it." Once: "Abandon urine-dyed clothes!" Ubayy: "Why? The Prophet and contemporaries wore them; Allah would reveal the prohibition." 'Umar: "True."

No Companion was afflicted by whispers; virtue never escaped the Prophet and Companions, Allah's favorites. The Prophet in our time: hate them; in Omar's time: they were punished.

Chapter 3: The Intention in Purification and Prayer

The intention (niyyah) is the inner resolve and determination to undertake an action. It resides exclusively in the heart, independent of words. Thus, the hadiths of the Prophet (peace and blessings be upon him) and his Companions confirm that they formed intentions for each relevant circumstance.

The artificial verbal formulas introduced to begin ablutions or prayer have sparked countless quarrels among those trapped by Satan's whispers. He relentlessly pushes them to pronounce them perfectly, leading the afflicted to stutter and laboriously repeat intention phrases, even though these words are not part of the prayer itself. The true intention is the heart's tacit commitment to the act. Sitting for ablutions inherently signals the intention to perform ablutions; standing for prayer signals the intention to pray.

Thus, the intention arises naturally from deliberate action, without artificial effort. Attempting to detach from it in voluntary acts is impossible. If Allah had made ablutions and prayer obligatory without intention, He would have imposed an unbearable burden. Doubting one's own intention borders on madness, for self-knowledge is axiomatic; how then can reason doubt its acts?

Imagine a person joining the Dhuhr prayer behind the imam: how could doubt assail him mid-act? Questioned on another matter, he retorts: "I'm busy; I'm going to pray Dhuhr." Surprisingly, those present understand his intention from the context. Sitting among the congregation awaiting prayer? His intention is clear. Standing for the iqamah with others? He prays. Advancing as imam? He leads the prayer.

If observers perceive the inner determination from external signs, how can one deny it internally? Accepting Satan's claim that he acts unintentionally confirms the devil, denies certainties, and strays from the Quran, Sunnah, and Companions' path.

Strangely, this doubt arises mid-prayer as the imam bows; fearing missing a rak'ah, he hastens the takbir to join—while claiming no intention was formed in an independent phase, but only rushed by distraction?

Why is it ignored by the Prophet, Companions, and successors, appearing only in minds influenced by Satan? Does he consider himself the devil's wise advisor? Does he ignore that demons attract only to evil?

What about the Prophet's and Muslims' voluntary prayers, incomplete? "An affliction," retort the afflicted. "In truth, it is accepting Satan's whispers; Allah does not forgive deviations from the Sunnah. Adam and Eve, for yielding once, were expelled from Paradise but forgiven for lack of precedence; you, warned of evil, path shown, have no excuse for straying from the Sunnah."

Ibn Taymiyyah: "Some invent ten innovations unknown to the Prophet and Companions: 'A'udhu billahi min al-shaytan al-rajim. I will perform the Dhuhr prayer at its time, prescribed by Allah, four rak'ahs, facing the Qibla.' Then, shaking the body and tilting the head, they cry like an enemy: 'Allahu Akbar!'"

The insinuation corrupting prayer: repetition of letters, e.g., takbir "ta-kkk," tashahhud "ta-hiyy"—potentially invalidating the prayer if pronounced by the imam, harming followers. Prayer, pinnacle of worship, is more harmful than a major sin. Minor deviations: makruh, deviation from Sunnah.

Raising the voice of the extremely afflicted invites ridicule—accumulating: obeying Satan, defying Sunnah, innovating in worship, self-torment/wasting time, diminishing rewards/missing benefits, exposing calumny, seducing the ignorant ("Beneficial, otherwise ignored—deficient Sunnah!").

Al-Ghazali et al.: "Roots of insinuation: ignorance of Sharia or madness—two grave defects."

Muslim: 'Uthman ibn Abi al-'As: "Messenger, Satan disturbs my prayer and troubles me." Prophet: "That is Khinzab's work; expel him, seek refuge, and spit three times to the left." "They did; Allah dispelled them."

Whispered: Khinzab's joy. Rest in Allah.

Chapter 4: Excessive Use of Water for Ablutions and Bathing

Ahmad reports in his Musnad, from Abdullah ibn Amr, that the Prophet passed by Sa'd while he was performing ablutions and said: "Do not waste." Sa'd asked: "Can one waste even water?" He replied: "Yes, even if you were performing ablutions in a river."

Ubayy ibn Ka'b reported that the Prophet said: "There is a Satan of ablutions called 'Al-Walhan'; beware of bad incitements to waste water."

A Bedouin came to the Messenger of Allah and asked about ablutions. He demonstrated (washing each body part) three times, then said: "This is the method of ablutions. Whoever does more has acted wrongly, transgressed the limit, and harmed himself."

Umm Sa'd reported that the Prophet (peace and blessings be upon him) said: "A saa' (measure) was once equal to a mudd (another measure), one-third of the mudd we use today; but today's saa' has become too large. A mudd of water suffices for ablutions, and a saa' for ghusl after major impurity. Some will exceed this rule, opposing my Sunnah. But those who adopt my Sunnah in their life will be in the Garden of Eden."

It is also reported in Sunan Abi Dawud, from Salim ibn Abu al-Ja'd following Jabir ibn Abdullah: "A mudd suffices for ablutions (wudu'), while a saa' suffices for ghusl after major impurity (janabah)." A man replied: "That would not suffice me." Jabir, furious, cried: "It sufficed someone better than you, and hairier!"

Aisha reported that she and the Prophet performed ablutions with a single vessel containing three mudds, or about.

Habib al-Ansari reported: "I heard 'Abbad ibn Tamim report, from my grandmother Umm Umarah, saying: 'The Prophet wanted to perform ablutions. A vessel containing water was brought to him.'"

Ibrahim an-Nakha'i said: "The Companions were more concerned than you not to waste water; they considered a third of a mudd sufficient for ablutions." This is a gross exaggeration; for a third of a mudd is a very small amount.

Anas ibn Malik said: "The Prophet performed ablutions with a mudd of water and ghusl with a saa', equivalent to three mudds of water."

Safinah said: "The Messenger of Allah took a bath with a saa' of water (after intercourse) and performed ablutions with a mudd."

Al-Qasim ibn Muhammad ibn Abu Bakr performed ablutions with half a mudd of water, or a little more.

Muhammad ibn 'Ajlan said: "Adequate knowledge of Allah's religion consists in knowing how to perform ablutions (wudu') correctly, using little water."

Abdullah ibn Mughaffal said: "I heard the Prophet say: In this community, there will be people who exceed limits in purification as in supplication."

Therefore, if you compare this hadith with Allah's words in this verse: {Indeed, Allah does not like transgressors.} (Al-Baqarah 2:190), you will know that Allah loves to see His servants worship Him, and you will understand that the ablution of the person under waswasah is not an accepted act of worship by Allah.

The corrupting aspect of waswasah is that it incites the person under its influence to use more water than necessary, especially if it is someone else's property, as in a public bath.

Chapter 5: Ignoring Insinuations Concerning the Breaking of Ablutions

It is appropriate to ignore any insinuation (waswasah) concerning the breaking of ablutions. If a person doubts having broken their ablutions—for example, wondering if a wind passed or a drop of urine escaped—they must base themselves on certainty and not on doubt. The fundamental principle in this matter is that purity established by certainty cannot be invalidated by doubt.

The Prophet (peace and blessings be upon him) said: "If one of you feels something in his belly and hesitates between whether it is a rumble or not, let him not leave the mosque until he hears a sound or smells an odor." This applies to prayer and any other situation: act according to certainty, and ignore doubt.

The scholars have ruled that if the doubt arises after ablutions, the person remains in a state of purity as long as there is no clear proof of breaking. Insisting on this doubt opens the door to Satan's whispers, who aims to multiply useless acts and exhaust the believer. The Sunnah teaches ease: once ablutions are performed correctly, they are valid until proven otherwise.

Thus, whoever is afflicted by these insinuations must remember Allah's word: {Allah intends for you ease and does not intend for you hardship.} (Al-Baqarah 2:185). Reject the doubt, resume your worship, and seek refuge in Allah from the stoned Satan.

Chapter 6: Acts Testifying to Religious Innovations

Acts that testify to religious innovations (bid'ah) are among the gravest traps of Satan, for they disguise themselves as piety while straying from the Sunnah. Satan incites the afflicted to multiply useless gestures in worship, such as repeating ablutions without valid reason or adding un prescribed formulas to prayer, believing this will bring them closer to Allah. Yet, these innovations nullify the reward and attract divine anger.

The Prophet (peace and blessings be upon him) warned: "Every innovation is misguidance, and every misguidance leads to the Fire." The Companions scrupulously followed the Sunnah without additions or omissions, avoiding the traps of doubt. Whoever introduces a novelty in religion, even from excess zeal, follows Satan in reality, who aims to corrupt pure acts.

Signs of these innovations include: excessive hesitation before takbir, repeating rak'ahs out of fear of error, or refusing group prayer due to imagined impurity fear. These are not legitimate precaution, but blameworthy deviation. The remedy is to rely on the Sunnah: perform worship as the Prophet taught, and ignore whispers that divert you.

Allah says: {This day I have perfected for you your religion and completed My favor upon you and have approved for you Islam as religion.} (Al-Ma'ida 5:3). Any addition thereafter is rejected bid'ah. Seek guidance in the Book and Sunnah, and let not Satan divert you from the straight path.

Chapter 7: Praying While Wearing Shoes

It is permissible, and even recommended, to perform prayer while wearing shoes, provided they are clean and free of visible impurity. The Prophet (peace and blessings be upon him) often prayed with his shoes on, as attested by the Companions. Abu Sa'id al-Khudri reported: "We prayed with the Messenger of Allah wearing our shoes, and he ordered us to remove them when he saw them dirty."

Satan whispers to the afflicted to doubt the purity of their shoes, inciting them to remove them for every prayer out of excess scruple, even if they are clean. This is a blameworthy innovation that burdens worship and contradicts the Sunnah, which advocates ease. If no impurity is apparent, consider them pure and pray with them, following the prophetic example.

The scholars said: "Praying in shoes is Sunnah, as long as they properly cover the feet and bear no impurity." Ignore the doubt; Allah has not burdened a soul beyond its capacity. Thus, this practice strengthens trust in the Sunnah and repels Satan's insinuations.

Chapter 8: The Sunnah of the Prophet Regarding Prayer Wherever He May Be

The Sunnah of the Prophet (peace and blessings be upon him) is clear: prayer can be performed wherever one is, as long as the place is pure and free of impurity. The Prophet prayed in mosques, homes, travels, and even on roofs or in gardens, without excessive restriction. He said: "The entire earth is a place of prostration for me and a means of purification."

Satan whispers to the afflicted to doubt the purity of every place, inciting them to seek perfect spots or postpone prayer due to imagined impurity fear. This contradicts the Sunnah, which teaches flexibility: pray on what is available and pure, without complication. If doubt arises about the ground's purity, base yourself on certainty; a pure place remains pure until proven otherwise.

The Companions followed this example: they prayed during expeditions and travels without excess. The scholars affirmed: "Prayer is valid everywhere except in cemeteries or stables out of respect." Ignore insinuations that turn worship into a burden; Allah has facilitated religion for His community.

Chapter 9: What to Do When Pre-Ejaculatory Fluid Touches Clothes?

When madhiy (pre-ejaculatory fluid) touches clothes, the Sunnah is clear: it suffices to wash the impure spot with water, without restarting full ablutions. The Prophet (peace and blessings be upon him) said: "Madhiy is an impurity; wash it wherever it is, but ablutions are required only for mani (semen)."

Satan whispers to the afflicted to doubt the purity of their entire clothes, inciting them to redo ghusl or change everything, even after simple washing. This is blameworthy exaggeration contradicting religion's ease. The scholars ruled: "Wash only the affected part; the rest remains pure."

Ignore this doubt: Allah distinguished minor impurities to lighten the burden. Follow the Sunnah: clean locally and resume worship without delay, seeking refuge from Satan's insinuations.

Chapter 10: The Use of Stones for Istinja (Post-Defecation Purification) and the Ruling on Pus

The use of stones for istinja (purification after defecation) is a simple prophetic practice: three pure stones suffice, or water if available. The Prophet (peace and blessings be upon him) said: "Whoever purifies with stones must use an odd number, three being sufficient." Regarding pus (qai'), it does not invalidate purity as long as it does not reach the anus or urethra; it is a local impurity requiring simple washing.

Satan whispers to the afflicted to doubt the number of stones or pus purity, inciting them to multiply gestures until exhaustion. This is exaggeration contrary to the Sunnah, which aims for ease. The scholars ruled: "Minor pus does not break ablutions; wash it locally without excess."

Ignore these insinuations: religion is easy, and Allah does not love transgressors. Follow the

Sunnah for serene purification, seeking refuge from Satan's traps.

Chapter 11: Carrying Children During Prayer

Carrying children during prayer is permissible, as long as they do not disturb concentration and are clean. The Prophet (peace and blessings be upon him) carried his grandson Hasan or Husayn on his shoulders during prayer, prolonging recitation to not disturb them. Ibn 'Abbas reported: "The Messenger of Allah prayed carrying a child."

Satan whispers to the afflicted to doubt the prayer's validity with a child, inciting them to put them down out of fear of imagined invalidity. This contradicts the Sunnah, which allows flexibility for fathers and mothers. The scholars said: "The prayer remains valid; the child does not break purity if dry."

Ignore the doubt: Allah appreciates balance between worship and family life. Carry them with confidence, following the prophetic example, and repel insinuations with faith.

Chapter 12: The Clothes of Polytheists

It is permissible to pray in clothes that belonged to polytheists, as long as they are pure and free of forbidden images or impurity. The Prophet (peace and blessings be upon him) wore non-Muslims' clothes without objection, and he said: "Seek your sustenance, and Allah will provide it for you; but do not seek it through disobedience."

Satan whispers to the afflicted to doubt such clothes' purity, inciting them to reject them out of excess scruple, even if washed. This is an innovation contrary to the Sunnah, which allows use of licit goods without excessive restriction. The scholars ruled: "Polytheists' clothes are pure if bearing no impurity; pray in them without doubt."

Ignore these insinuations: religion promotes well-being, not anguish. Use what is available, following the prophetic example, and seek refuge from Satan's isolating traps.

Chapter 13: Praying with a Small Amount of Blood That Does Not Flow

Performing prayer with a small amount of blood that does not flow is permissible, as long as the quantity does not exceed the size of a dirham (about 5 cm^2). The Prophet (peace and blessings be upon him) said: "Trim the nails and mustache; this is part of the fitrah." And in a similar hadith: "Prayer is accepted despite a small amount of blood, for difficulty is not in blood that does not flow."

Satan whispers to the afflicted to doubt the prayer's validity, inciting excessive washing or postponing prayer out of fear of imagined invalidity. This contradicts the Sunnah, which distinguishes flowing blood (breaking purity) from static (not invalidating if minimal). The scholars ruled: "A small non-flowing blood spot does not prevent prayer; ignore the doubt and pray."

Ignore these insinuations: Allah has lightened religion for His community. Follow the Sunnah by covering the spot if possible, but without exaggeration, and seek refuge from Satan's traps that turn purity into torment.

Chapter 14: Accepting Food from the People of the Book

Accepting food from the People of the Book (Jews and Christians) is permissible, as long as it contains no forbidden impurity like meat not slaughtered according to Sharia or pork. Allah says: {The food of those who were given the Scripture is lawful for you and your food is lawful for them.} (Al-Ma'ida 5:5). The Prophet (peace and blessings be upon him) accepted invitations from Jews and ate their food, as reported by Anas ibn Malik.

Satan whispers to the afflicted to doubt this food's purity, inciting them to refuse it out of excess scruple, even if halal. This is a deviation from the Sunnah, which encourages trade and conviviality with the People of the Book without excessive suspicion. The scholars ruled: "Accept it if known pure; doubt does not invalidate the permissible."

Ignore these insinuations: religion promotes moderation and trust in liciety. Share meals following the prophetic example, and seek refuge from Satan's traps that isolate and harden hearts.

Chapter 15: The Similarity Between Polytheism and Forbidding the Permissible

The similarity between polytheism and forbidding what is permissible is striking: just as associating partners with Allah is the greatest sin, forbidding what Allah has permitted out of excess scruple is a minor form of unbelief. The Prophet (peace and blessings be upon him) said: "Whoever forbids what is permissible has invented a lie against Allah."

Satan whispers to the afflicted to consider halal as haram, like doubting the purity of permissible food or clean clothing. This resembles polytheism, for it attributes to creation a sanctity or impurity not intended by the Creator. The scholars ruled: "Forbidding the permissible by innovation is a grave deviation, akin to shirk in its effect on faith."

Ignore these insinuations: Allah said {And do not say about what your tongues assert of untruth, "This is lawful and this is unlawful," to invent falsehood about Allah. Indeed, those who invent falsehood about Allah will not succeed.} (An-Nahl 16:116). Respect divine limits without addition; true faith is in balance, and seek refuge from Satan who distorts truth.

Chapter 16: Insinuations in the Pronunciation of Letters

Here is what the scholars said on this matter: Abu al-Faraj al-Juzy said: "Iblis (Satan) has disturbed some believers in their pronunciation of letters. They were seen sometimes pronouncing the word twice, saying: al-hamdu - al-hamdu, exceeding the prayer's terms, and they were seen intensifying the pronunciation of the letter 'd' in the word: 'al-maghdoub.' " He said: "I saw people trying to pronounce the letter 'd' intensely, and they ended up spitting. Iblis diverts them from understanding the recitation by making them focus on the correctness of pronunciation. These are the effects of Iblis's waswasah."

Muhammad ibn Qutaybah said about the problem of Quranic recitation: "In the past, people recited the Quran in their own language (Arabic). Then came people from non-Arab lands who did not master the language of the Quran. They skimmed over many letters and thus perverted the rules of recitation. Among them was a man reputed for his piety; yet, I have never heard a more hesitant recitation."

He confused letters, pronouncing the first correctly and the next wrongly. He introduced other ways of pronouncing certain letters, different from the recitation of the Arab natives of the Arabian Peninsula. He imposed on his students his difficult and confused recitation, while Allah and His Prophet facilitated everything for the community.

The most astonishing is that he imposed his recitation on people when leading them in prayer, forcing them to pray behind him. When Ibn 'Uyaynah saw someone praying using the recitation taught by this man, or when he himself was behind an imam reciting the Quran with this confused recitation, he (Ibn 'Uyaynah) considered the prayer must be repeated, and many scholars agreed with his opinion, such as Bishr ibn al-Harith and Imam Ahmad ibn Hanbal.

It was not the Prophet's recitation, nor that of the Companions and their successors, nor that of the experts in the matter. It was rather simple and easy.

Al-Khallal said in "Al-Jami'": "Abu Abdullah said: 'I do not like this man's recitation.'"

It was reported that Ibn al-Mubarak forbade Ar-Rabi' ibn Anas from reciting the Quran in this manner.

Al-Fadl ibn Zayad said: "A man said to Abu Abdillah: 'What should be avoided in recitation?' He replied: 'Contracting letters and fragmenting words, which was not known in any Arabic dialect.'"

Al-Hasan ibn Muhammad ibn al-Harith asked him: "Do you hate a man learning such a recitation?" He replied: "I hate it greatly; it is an innovated recitation." He hated it so much that it made him furious.

It is reported that Ibn Sunayd was asked about this recitation and replied: "I hate it greatly." He was asked: "What do you dislike so much?" He replied: "It is an unprecedented recitation, which no one had done before."

Abdurrahman ibn Mahdi declared: "If I had to perform prayer behind an imam reciting this recitation, I would repeat it."

Ahmad ibn Hanbal said that he would also repeat the prayer behind an imam reciting such a prayer.

Another version reports that he would not repeat such a prayer.

The important point here is that the scholars disapproved of these recitations with intensified and innovated pronunciation of the Quran's letters.

Whoever reflects on the Prophet's teachings will clearly see that all aspects of waswasah (misinterpretations) in the pronunciation of the Quran's letters are not part of his Sunnah.

Chapter 17: Refutation of the Excuses of Those Affected by Insinuations

They say: "What we do is only precaution, not waswasah."

We say: "Call it what you will. We ask you only: 'Is it in accordance with the Sunnah of the Prophet or his Companions? Or is it the opposite?'"

"If you claim it is in accordance with the Sunnah, it is a lie. You must renounce this claim and recognize that it contradicts the Sunnah; consequently, you should not call it precaution." This is comparable to someone committing an illegal act and labeling it otherwise, just as alcoholic beverages have different names, and usury is called commerce.

It is appropriate to know that a beneficial precaution that earns Allah's reward consists in acting in accordance with the Prophet's Sunnah and abstaining from everything opposing it.

Likewise, some people, in times of conflict, hastily pronounce divorce, a practice contested by scholars regarding its legality. This includes forced divorce, divorce pronounced by an intoxicated person, divorce by niyyah (divorce by mere intention), deferred divorce (planned divorce with a fixed date), divorce by oath (loan divorce), and many other types of divorce widely contested by scholars. If the mufti (judge) accepts divorce by mere convention, without any proof, and declares: "This is a precaution against any illicit sexual relation," then he has actually ignored the true meaning of precaution in this matter; for he prohibits it for one and legalizes it for another. Thus, one may ask: "Where is the precaution in such a judgment?"

In contrast, if he does not pronounce divorce until a majority of the community's scholars have ruled on it (based on the Quran and the Prophet's Sunnah), it can be considered precautionary. This was the opinion of Imam

Ahmad regarding divorce pronounced by a drunk man.

Shaykh Ibn Taymiyyah said: "Precaution is a good thing, as long as it does not lead the mufti to contradict the Sunnah. If it does, the 'precautionary measure' consists then in setting aside this 'precaution.'"

This is the response to their arguments and excuses, supported by the Prophet's hadiths: "Whoever avoids these suspicious things preserves his religion and honor," "Keep away from what makes you doubt and turn to what does not make you doubt," and "Sin is what troubles a person's soul." These hadiths constitute convincing proof of the invalidation of waswasah.

It is in suspicious things that truth collides with falsehood, the permissible with the prohibited, without any proof brought to either party. That is why the Prophet guided us to avoid what is suspicious and retain only what is clear and evident.

Al-Waswas's (Satan's) goal is to sow confusion in the Muslim, making him believe that his action is in accordance with the Sunnah or that it is a bid'ah (an innovation).

The clear and evident path is to follow the Prophet's path and the directives he established for his community, in words and deeds.

Whoever follows the path of suspicion in his life has indeed neglected the Sunnah and adopted the blameworthy innovation (bid'ah); he has abstained from pleasing Allah and accepted what displeases Him. He has distanced himself from Allah, for the only way to draw closer to Him is to obey His commands, not to satisfy one's own desires.

As for the date from which the Messenger of Allah abstained, saying: "I fear it might be charity"—since it was forbidden for the Prophet (peace and blessings be upon him) and his family to eat charity—it was a precaution against suspicious things, where the permissible is confused with the prohibited.

For he found the date at his home, and since they used to bring them, he gave it to the poor who deserved it. However, his family also regularly brought dates, so he did not know which category this one belonged to. That is why he abstained from eating it. This hadith incites caution and vigilance regarding suspicious things, but has nothing to do with those prone to waswasah. Their argument is simply invalid.

Regarding your argument about Imam Malik's ruling, according to which, for a person who announced a divorce without remembering if it was the first or the third, one should consider it the third out of precaution, we reply: "Indeed, that was Malik's opinion. But does this have to constitute proof contrary to the opinion of Shafi'i, Abu Hanifa, Imam Ahmad, or all those who do not share his opinion on this point?

Should everyone renounce his opinion and submit to his?"

This opinion is not related to waswasah, but his argument is: "Divorce entails the prohibition of marriage with the wife (she does not become permissible for her husband again), but rij'ah (remarriage with his ex-wife, provided it is not the third divorce) lifts this prohibition. As Imam Malik said: 'The reason for the prohibition is established: divorce.' However, he had doubts regarding remarriage, for if it was not the definitive divorce (i.e., the third), the prohibition could be lifted by the possibility of remarriage. But if it is the third and final divorce, remarriage with his ex-wife is impossible, and the prohibition is then established.'"

The majority of scholars said: "Marriage being certain, its annulment is doubtful, for return to his wife (rij'ah) is possible; a fact that does not prevent remarriage. Consequently, remarriage is maintained until confirmation of annulment."

If you say: "The prohibition of remarriage is certain, so its permissibility is doubtful," we reply: "Remarriage is not forbidden for you, and you thus legalize sexual relations becoming remarried, if the intention is that which desires it."

If you say: "It is forbidden, and rij'ah occurred only with intention at the time of sexual relation," we reply: "This is a weak argument that does not even support your opinion."

The oath sworn in case of divorce on any element (like two seeds in a nut, etc.) of which the swearer is not certain, and whose result differs from what he thought, is not broken according to many scholars.

Likewise, if the issue is not clear and remains unknown, marriage remains certain and should not be questioned by doubt.

Imam Malik issued a ruling contested by other scholars. According to this ruling, divorce can be pronounced in case of doubt on an oath, in the same way as when there is doubt as to the nature of the divorce (first, second, or definitive), as mentioned above, and also in case of doubt concerning a divorced wife. If her husband announces having divorced one of his wives, but forgets which one, the divorce is then justified. In other words, when a man swears on the identity of a wife while having doubts, his oath is considered broken due to his state of doubt at the time of the oath.

The oath is broken when the result differs from what was initially expected. If it is a request, the oath is broken when the person does what he committed by oath. If it rests on information, the oath is broken when this information proves false.

Malik added another condition that can lead to breaking an oath (doubt at the time of swearing), whether the oath leads to truth or not.

The ruling is therefore precautionary in case of oath breaking (hanath), due to the doubt that persists regarding its validity. Indeed, when a person swears, he may then doubt having broken it or not. The Maliki scholars would then order his separation from his wife.

Is this ruling obligatory or recommended? There are two opinions: that of Ibn al-Qasim and that of Malik.

Malik considered it a continuation of marriage.

Ibn al-Qasim said: "Since the state of marriage became doubtful, the husband must be separated from his wife."

However, the majority of scholars said that he should not divorce her, and that it is not even recommended for him to do so; for the rule of the Sharia states: doubt is not a sufficiently solid basis to remove the initially known element; what is certain cannot be removed except by something more certain or equal to it.

Chapter 18: The Ruling on Contested Divorce

Regarding the man who divorced one of his wives and forgot her, or who divorced a woman without mentioning her name, the scholars differed in opinion on the ruling:

According to Abu Hanifa, Shafi'i, Thawri, and Hammad: "He chooses the one he wants and pronounces divorce with her. As for the one he divorced and forgot, he must not approach any of his wives, but provide for their needs until the situation is clarified. If he dies before discovering which of his wives he divorced and forgot, Abu Hanifa says that all his wives must then share the inheritance of the latter."

Shafi'i said: "Marriage must be suspended until the spouses have reconciled." The Maliki school says: "If a husband divorces an unspecified wife, saying: 'You are divorced,' but not knowing which one, his statement applies to all. If he divorces a specified wife, then forgets which one, he must abstain from any marriage with them until he remembers. If he delays, a deadline must be set for him; otherwise, he must divorce all. If he announces to his wives: 'One of you is divorced,' without intentionally specifying, they must all be repudiated."

Imam Ahmad said: "He chooses by drawing lots among them in both cases." This statement was reported by a group of his companions, and his narration relied on the authority of Ali and Ibn 'Abbas. The unanimous opinion of this school is that there is no difference between the unspecified divorced wife and the forgotten one.

Ibn Qudamah said: "He chooses by drawing lots the unspecified wife. As for the one he forgot, he must abstain from any contact with his other wives until the identity of the one he divorced is known, and continue to provide for all their needs. If he dies, the drawing of lots will decide the distribution of the inheritance among them."

Ismaïl ibn Ahmad reported, from Ahmad, that the drawing of lots should not be used for a forgotten wife, but it can serve to decide the sharing of the inheritance. Ismaïl said: "I asked Ahmad about a man who had divorced one of his wives, but did not know which one." He replied: "I strongly advise against proceeding with a divorce by drawing lots." I asked: "And if the man dies?" He replied: "I recommend the drawing of lots, for it is used to determine who inherits."

Regarding doubts on purity, the legal opinion of Al-Hasan, Ibrahim an-Nakha'i, and Imam Malik (in one of his hadiths), regarding a person who doubts the validity of his ablutions, is that he must redo them out of precaution and not perform prayer in a state of doubt about his purity. This question is widely debated by the scholars.

The majority of scholars, including Shafi'i, Ahmad, Abu Hanifa and their companions, as well as Imam Malik in another narration, said that he should not redo his ablutions, but pray with the ablutions of which he is certain, even if he has doubts about their validity.

They supported their opinion on a narration from Abu Hurayrah who said: "The Messenger of Allah (peace and blessings be upon him) said: 'If one of you feels abdominal pain but doubts the origin of his secretions, let him not leave the mosque unless he hears a sound or smells an odor.'" This applies to prayer or other acts.

The adherents of the first opinion affirm: the state of prayer (Salah) is confirmed by uncertainty, while doubt persists regarding the validity of ablutions (wudu'). Consequently, as long as one is uncertain of their validity, one should not perform prayer with doubt.

Others would say that it is a Salah founded on a state of known purity, whose validity is doubtful. Thus, one should not dwell on the doubt as long as certainty remains. Likewise, if one doubts the purity of his clothes or body, he should not wash them, for that would amount to entering prayer with doubt.

They established a distinction between the two based on two interpretations: first, avoiding impurity is not a condition, and consequently, its intention (niyyah) is not obligatory. It is rather a precautionary measure, which never existed at the origin. In contrast, ablutions (wudu') are a fundamental element; how then to doubt their certainty?

Second: before performing his ablutions (wudu'), he was in a state of ritual impurity (after using the toilet, etc.), which was his initial state. Consequently, if he doubts the validity of his ablutions, he returns to his initial state; the authenticity is therefore not linked to impurity or any other form of impurity.

Others affirm: the principle of impurity is abolished by the certainty of purity, which becomes the original state or principle; thus, in case of doubt on purity, we refer to it for decision. How does this compare to waswasah, prohibited by religion, both from the perspective of reason and tradition?

What to do when one ignores the location of an impurity on his clothes? Regarding the argument that if someone does not recognize the location of an impurity on his clothes, he should wash everything, it is not a matter of waswasah (religious obsession). It is rather fulfilling an obligation. In this case, he must wash the impure part of his clothes; but since he does not know the place, he must wash the entire garment to fulfill his obligation.

Chapter 19: Confusion in Determining the Purity or Impurity of Clothes

This is a controversial issue among scholars.

Imam Malik, in one of his hadiths, and Imam Ahmad said that in this situation, it is appropriate to pray with different clothes to ensure their purity. However, the majority of scholars, including Abu Hanifa, Shafi'i, and Malik in another hadith, said that one must examine the clothes and perform a prayer with one of the two; this examination is similar to searching for the Qibla.

Al-Muzni and Abu Thawr affirmed that it is better to pray naked than dressed in impure clothes, for it is prohibited to pray in impure clothes; consequently, if one is unable to cover himself with pure clothes, the obligation to cover is lifted. But this is the least favorable opinion.

The clearest and most favorable opinion is the one that consists of examining one's clothes, depending on the number of clean clothes; this was the opinion of Shaykh Ibn Taymiyyah. As for Ibn 'Ugayl, he said that if there were many clothes, one should trust his intuition, but if there were only a few, he should examine them all.

Shaykh Ibn Taymiyyah said: "Avoiding impurity is a necessity; thus, if someone examined his clothes and estimated that one of them was pure, he must pray with these clothes. His prayer should not be invalidated due to doubt."

The opinion of Abu Thawr (praying naked in case of doubt on the purity of his clothes) is totally invalid; for even if someone is certain of the impurity of his clothes, his prayer performed with them is more appreciated by Allah than praying naked, exposing his private parts to people.

In any case, this does not fall under the type of blameworthy waswasah.

Doubt about the purity of vessels used for ablutions is not a matter of waswasah, and scholars have had very divergent opinions on this subject.

Imam Ahmad said: "Then perform tayammum and do not use water contained in suspect vessels." In another version, he said: "One must pour out this water and perform tayammum to be certain not to have pure water."

Abu Hanifa said: "When the number of pure vessels exceeds that of impure ones, it is appropriate to examine which one to use; but if they are equal or fewer in number, it is not necessary to examine them." This opinion was also shared by some companions of Imam Ahmad, such as Abu Bakr, Ibn Shaqilla, and An-Najjad, the pious scholar who reported many hadiths from Imam Ahmad.

Ash-Shafi'i and some Maliki scholars affirmed that it was appropriate to examine the vessels in all situations.

A group of scholars, including our shaykh, said that ablutions should be performed using any vessel, starting from the principle that water becomes impure only when it changes taste or color.

Al-Hasan, Ibrahim an-Nakha'i, and Malik (in a narration): Abu Hurayrah reported that the Prophet said: "If one of you feels abdominal pain but doubts the origin of his secretions, let him not leave the mosque unless he hears a sound or smells an odor." This applies to prayer or other acts.

Confusion regarding the direction of the Qibla: The scholars said that if one is confused about the direction of the Qibla, he must follow his own judgment, at the place where he is, then perform the Salah.

A scholar issued an unusual opinion affirming that in such a situation, it is appropriate to perform four prayers (Salats) in four directions. This is contrary to the Sunnah; however, its author based his judgment on confusion regarding the purity of clothes, but this opinion remains unusual and should be set aside.

Chapter 20: Confusion Related to Forgetting a Prayer Without Knowing Which One

Scholars have divergent opinions on this issue.

First opinion: Ahmad, Malik, Ash-Shafi'i, Abu Hanifa, and Ishaq said that one must pray the five prayers (Salahs), for there is no other way to be certain of having performed the correct prayer.

Second opinion: it is appropriate to perform a four-rak'ah prayer, with the intention of compensating for the forgotten one, but one must sit for tahiyyah in all rak'ahs; this was the opinion of Al-Awza'i, Zufar ibn al-Hudhayl, and Muhammad ibn Mugatil from the Hanafi school.

Third opinion: to compensate for a forgotten but unknown Salah, it is appropriate to pray one Fajr, one Maghrib, and one of the four-rak'ah prayers, with the intention of covering the forgotten one; this was the opinion of Sufyan ath-Thawri and Muhammad ibn al-Hasan.

As for Abdullah ibn Ahmad, he said: "I heard my father being asked: 'What to do if a person who is reminded that he forgot a prayer prays two rak'ahs, does the tashahhud, intending it to be the morning prayer, but without yet doing the salam; then stands up, prays one rak'ah, does the tashahhud, intending it to cover a Maghrib prayer; then stands up, prays a fourth rak'ah, does the tashahhud, intending it to cover a Dhuhr or Asr prayer, and ends with salam?' My father replied: 'This would compensate and cover his forgotten prayer.'"

To invalidate the proofs of those under the influence of waswasah: If someone has a doubt in his Salah, he must base his decision on the certainty of his mind.

Regarding the prohibition of consuming game, if one has doubts about the cause of its death (injury, drowning) or prohibits its consumption if his own dogs were crossed with others', the Prophet ordered that in such cases, consumption be prohibited, for one doubts the permissibility of its consumption, while the animal was initially prohibited. Consequently, one should not legalize its consumption in case of doubt (subject to its permissibility), which is contrary to the principle that the animal was initially permissible; indeed, doubt does not make an animal prohibited. This is comparable to the situation where one buys water, food, or clothes without knowing their nature (their permissibility) and doubts their purity; if the element is initially permissible, ignore the doubt.

For example: if someone receives meat without knowing its origin, nor knowing if the animal was slaughtered according to Sharia, it is permissible to consume it, given the difficulty in verifying its provenance. Aisha asked the Prophet: "O Messenger of Allah, Arabs from the countryside bring us meat, but we do not know if they invoked Allah's name before slaughtering the animal." He replied: "Invoke Allah's name and eat."

In the second example concerning water, food, and clothes, the original state of these things was pure; so one only doubts the existence of some form of impurity, and consequently, does not take this doubt into account.

Chapter 21: The Insinuations of Ibn 'Umar Regarding Ablutions

Regarding what some (under the influence of waswasah) say about Ibn 'Umar and Abu Hurayrah, it was a criticism specific to them, and no Companion shared Ibn 'Umar's opinion on this point. Ibn 'Umar himself said: "I am under the influence of waswasah, so do not take me as an example."

The apparent interpretation of the Shafi'i school and Ahmad's is that it is not recommended to wash the inside of the eyes during ablutions, even if it presents no danger; for it has never been reported that the Prophet (peace and blessings be upon him) practiced this gesture, nor that he ordered it to anyone. The Prophet's ablutions were reported by many Companions, such as Uthman, Ali, Abdullah ibn Zayd, Rubayyi bint Mu'awwidh, and others; none of them mentioned that he washed the inside of the eyes.

Regarding the obligation to wash the eyes in a state of major impurity (janabah), two hadiths from Imam Ahmad are reported. The correct hadith, shared by the majority of scholars, indicates that there is no obligation. Consequently, it is not necessary to wash the inside of the eyes to purify them, for it risks aggravating the situation more than cleaning it.

The Shafi'i and Hanafi schools affirm that it is necessary to wash them; as they are rarely affected by impurity, it is not difficult to clean them.

Some scholars among Imam Ahmad's companions exaggerated further by suggesting that the eyes should be cleaned during ablutions. This opinion is to be rejected, for the correct opinion is that it is not obligatory to wash the eyes, whether for ablutions, after janabah, or for any other form of impurity.

Regarding Abu Hurayrah's interpretation, it was specific to him, and many scholars contested it. This issue was qualified as an extension of al-ghurrah, although al-ghurrah is particularly linked to the face.

There are two narrations from Ahmad on this issue: First: it is recommended to prolong the ablutions, and this was the opinion of Abu Hanifa and Shafi'i, as well as Abu al-Barakaat Ibn Taymiyyah and others.

Second: it is not recommended, and this was the opinion of the Maliki school, and the choice of our shaykh, Abu al-'Abbas.

Those who recommended prolonging ablutions supported their view on the hadith reported by Abu Hurayrah who said: "The Messenger of Allah said: 'In a believer, adornment will reach the places where ablutions stop.'"

Those who rejected this recommendation said: "The Prophet said: 'Allah has fixed limits; do not exceed them.'" Allah prescribed, during ablutions, to limit the washing of arms and feet to the elbow and ankle; consequently, one should not go beyond during ablutions.

Moreover, it has never been reported that the Prophet exceeded these limits during his ablutions; the origin of this exaggeration lies therefore in waswasah, which incites to perform this act as a form of worship to draw closer to Allah. However, worshiping Allah as it should be consists in following the Sunnah of His Prophet, not exaggerating in any act.

Neither the Prophet nor his Companions ever exaggerated in their ablutions, and he once said: "O people, beware of excess in religion."

The hadith of Abu Hurayrah mentioned above was reported by Nu'aym al-Mujmir, who said: "I do not know if the words: 'Whoever is able to prolong the washing of his private parts during ablutions may do so' are from the Prophet or from Abu Hurayrah."

As for the hadith of adornment, the adornment of embellishment is that applied to its place; if it exceeds its place, it is no longer adornment.

Chapter 22: Response to Those Who Claim That Insinuations Are Better Than Leniency

You claimed that being under the influence of waswasah (and acting beyond the norms or limits set by the Prophet) was preferable to negligence and lack of seriousness. Yet, such acts pertain to negligence, exaggeration, excess, laxity, extravagance, and avarice, and Allah has prohibited these two behaviors in many Quranic verses, when He says: "And do not extend your hand fully to spend [causing] you to become poor and in need."

"Do not spend wastefully, like a spendthrift. [And those who, when they spend, are neither extravagant nor stingy, but hold a medium [way] between those [extremes].]"

"Eat and drink, but do not waste."

"Do not make your hand [too] tight in your garment lest you become blaming and insolvent." (Al-Isra' 17:29). "And do not spend wastefully. Indeed, the wasteful are brothers of the devils." (Al-Isra' 17:27). "[Those who] when they spend, are neither extravagant nor stingy, but hold a medium [way] between those [extremes]." (Al-Furqan 25:67). "Eat and drink, but be not excessive. Indeed, He likes not those who commit excess." (Al-A'raf 7:31).

Allah's religion lies between excess and negligence, and the best are those who are in the middle, avoiding the negligence of the heedless and guarding against mingling with excesses and transgressors. For Allah has made the Muslim Ummah a balanced community, which constitutes a just choice, by its median position between a reprehensible state (excess and negligence) and justice, which represents a middle way.

These were the stratagems of Satan and his influence within our Ummah, so that sincere Muslims may know the merit of possessing knowledge (ilm) and faith (iman), and thus understand all of Allah's blessings upon them.

By His blessings, Allah guides whom He wills among those who seek truth within this Ummah, for success and right guidance come from Allah.

This is the conclusion of this book; thus, everything just in this book comes from Allah alone, and everything false in this book comes from the author and Satan.

I ask Allah to make this endeavor a sincere effort, seeking His approval, and I ask Him to grant us refuge with Him from the evil that is in us and in our actions. I ask Him to grant us success in accomplishing what pleases Him; He is near and responds to the prayers of His faithful servants.

Praise be to Allah, Lord of the Worlds; and may His prayer be upon the Prophet Muhammad, his family, and all his Companions.

www.ingramcontent.com/pod-product-compliance
Lightning Source LLC
Chambersburg PA
CBHW052139270326
41930CB00012B/2953
9781222269611